Transitions of Life
Walking with Destiny

Gary Heyes

ISBN:1515073688
ISBN-13:9781515073680

DEDICATION

I would like to dedicate this to Sheila my lovely bride of
30 years. She has walked with me through many
transitions and has always been a source of strength
and encouragement to our family.
Sheila, I love you with all my heart.

CONTENTS

ACKNOWLEDGMENTS

Thank you to my wife who always encourages me
Thank you to Mary Ann Meyer & Charlene Groen for editing & helpful insights
Thank you Melissa Heyes for the cover photo
Thank you for those who encouraged me to write

TRUST THE GPS!

A few years ago on a family vacation, I decided to purchase a new GPS navigation system. As we headed home from Myrtle Beach the GPS started giving me directions. Throughout the drive I would be asked to leave the highway and follow alternate routes (this was supposedly the faster way home). After having done this a few times my wife and I began to question the GPS and stayed on the route we were currently on as it didn't make sense for us to go off the path we were on, we heard the annoying re-calculating voice many times. On one particular occasion; we decided to not to follow the GPS instructions and ended up in a 30-minute traffic jam in pouring rain. What I didn't know was that my GPS came with the capability to know when traffic was heavy or jammed and it would re-route us. We began to laugh and repeat to each other "TRUST the GPS; listen to her voice." I'm happy to say we made it home and have continued to listen to the GPS.

This book is like a GPS navigation system; I hope to be able to offer some guidance in our journey through the transitions that come to our lives. Some of the transitions we will go through will be awesome; others will cause us to question what is going on and what is God up to.

Transition has been defined as:

- A passage from one state, stage, subject or place to another.
- A movement, development or evolution from one form, stage or style to another www.dictionary.com

Change is never easy, but it is required if we are going to walk into the destiny God has for us. I'm writing to help anyone who is about to go through or is going through a transition, a change or even a course correction. I want to help navigate the various transitions we face, discuss the emotions, decisions and obstacles we will encounter as we walk through this unique time and hopefully offer some steps to help along the way.

Throughout my life, I have experienced various transitions: career shifts, family tragedy and deaths, pastoring and not pastoring, leading people, managing departments, starting and running a business, struggling with infertility, raising a teenager and now becoming an empty nester - all the while seeing the hand of God come through time and time again.

I've learned through it all GOD IS IN CONTROL!

Would you take a moment to think on this thought? God is in Control!

- HE UPHOLDS ALL THINGS BY HIS WORD
- HE GOVERNS ALL EVENTS BY HIS WISDOM
- HE DIRECTS EVERYTHING TO ITS APPOINTED END
- HE DOES THIS, ALL THE TIME, IN EVERY CIRCUMSTANCE
- HE DOES IT ALWAYS FOR HIS OWN GLORY

Will you trust God with the details of your life?

I hope by the end of this book you will be able to have some tools to navigate this season and move forward into your destiny, the destiny and purpose you were created for and that your heart will be at peace and clean, having been able to remove the things that could or are holding you back.

God has a great plan for each and everyone of us.

Philippians 1:6 states:

There has never been the slightest doubt in my mind that the God who started this great work in you would keep at it and bring it to a flourishing finish on the very day Christ Jesus appears. MSG

HOLY SPIRIT INTENTIONS

Recently for my fiftieth birthday, a group of 45 friends, some life-long, gathered at a local restaurant to celebrate with me. They presented me with quite a beautiful and expensive watch. What they didn't know is that this watch had a significant impact on me. It symbolized what God was doing in my life and is a constant reminder that His timing is perfect and always right.

After spending 16 years as a staff pastor at a great church, I was recently interrupted by the Lord to move in a new direction, to start a business and travel speaking and ministering at various churches that I'm connected with.

I am beginning a new part of my journey—a journey that started over 30 years ago as I bowed my knee to receive Jesus into my heart. What a journey it has been!

Transitions are a part of the journey.

Throughout our lives, every one of us will go through multiple times of transition: a rite of passage, a stage of life and movement from one place to another. Transitions are and should be regular occurrences in our walk of faith.

A transition is the time in-between where we are and where we are going. It's a unique time that requires wisdom and grace to walk through. It's a place in which we need to guard our heart (Proverbs 4:23) for it is a place of sensitivity and change.

Matthew 11:28-30 states: *"Are you tired? Worn out? Burned out on religion? Come to me. Get away with me and you'll recover your life. I'll show you how to take a real rest. Walk with me and work with me—watch how I do it. Learn the* ***unforced rhythms of grace****. I won't lay anything heavy or ill-fitting on you. Keep company with me and you'll learn to live freely and lightly." MSG*

We all need to learn the UNFORCED RHYTHMS of GRACE. When grace is working in our lives things go smoother, it's less stressful and there is a special peace that comes over everything we engage in.

GRACE is the divine influence upon the heart and its reflection in the life

GRACE has the power to take us to where we are unable to go ourselves.

GRACE is God doing for us what we are incapable of doing ourselves.

GRACE has a rhythm that we all need to allow to shape our lives.

GOD has a great plan for our lives. Part of that plan is for us to recover life.

Sometimes as we are navigating this journey we can lose the real meaning and purpose of life itself.

I believe transitions are God sent interruptions for us to recalibrate our lives and recover God's original intent.

"God's intent is not to shake us or to break us, but to bring us to new levels of life in HIM. To break through to a higher level of life requires power, supernatural power that humans, in our own strength, are incapable of producing." Joey Bonifacio – The Promise No One Wants.

God's intent is to get us to a place in HIM where Our Heart takes captive or is captured by His promises. That we hear in such a way as to listen with the intent to act!

As we get away with HIM - we recover our lives, we begin to find real rest, nothing is too heavy for us to bare and we begin to live freely and lightly.

Our task is to walk with HIM, work with HIM, to watch how HE does life and to learn the unforced rhythms of grace.

Rhythm is an important piece to the life we live, we've all noticed when someone is on the dance floor with no rhythm, or listened to a song that isn't quite in sync. It makes us uncomfortable at the very least.

The Lord Jesus wants us to walk with a rhythm to our life, He gave the Holy Spirit to us so that HE would help establish this rhythm of grace and not be burdened with struggles and stress.

If you're a believer, the Holy Spirit intends to do at least two things:

1. **To bring us to a place where WE TRUST God for everything and with everything!**

God wants us to recognize that He is in control. Our lives are in His hands. Psalm 139:5 – "*You have hedged me behind and before, and laid Your hand upon me.*" *NKJV*

Psalm 139 is a great example of the life that is under God's control, wherever we go HE is there, His thoughts are always toward us and He is willing to lead and guide us. Once we acknowledge and surrender, then the real journey can begin.

2. **To bring us to a place where HE can TRUST us!**

He wants to trust us with His glory, favour and promises. To do that, we need to be in a place where we are able to handle what He wants to give or reveal to us.

Transitions happen. Their design is to move us to a better place, to bring us to a greater place of increase and fruitfulness in our lives.

Transitions are meant to bring a **level of change** that will produce new things in our spirit and ultimately a demonstration in the natural world.

We need to be willing to grow and allow the Holy Spirit to change us by captivating our desires and will into a place of dependence upon Him for our guidance, sustenance and experience.

The Holy Spirit wants to invade our daily moments to direct us toward His purpose for our lives. He wants to guide us each step of the way. Our journey is a personal journey engaged with the Godhead to help us be fulfilled in what we were created for.

The Holy Spirit wants to be our source in everything we face.

Transitions are unique times when we are encouraged to place our trust in a great God who cares deeply for us and wants to see us experience everything that He has provided for our journey.

Will we be open to be stretched and increased, to receive what He wants to give us?

The things that He has prepared for us God reveals them to us by His Spirit.

That is what the Scriptures mean when it says:

No eye has seen, no ear has heard, and no mind has imagined what God has prepared for those who love him."

But it was to us that God revealed these things by his Spirit. For his Spirit searches out everything and shows us God's deep secrets. No one can know a person's thoughts except that persons own spirit, and no one can know God's thoughts except God's own Spirit. And we have received God's Spirit (not the world's spirit), so we can know the wonderful things God has freely given us. 1 Corinthians 2:9-12 NKJV

Let's all decide today to allow God's wonderful GRACE to touch every part of our lives, through each transition we are walking through.

Questions to Ponder

1. Where can you see God's grace working in your life?

2. How have you felt forced in your life?

3. What areas do you need to learn to move in the unforced rhythms of grace?

WALKING WITH DESTINY

In his life, Winston Churchill, the great British leader during the Second World War, was involved in many political areas. On the http://www.winston-churchill-leadership.com site, a chart of his achievements lists fourteen areas he was involved in before he became Prime Minister. One of his achievements is listed as the "Wilderness Years." I would like to suggest that many of us have felt like there have been times we could call "Wilderness years!" Nothing is lost with God! He wants to take all of our experiences and use them for his purpose and glory in our lives.

On the evening that he became Prime Minister, to answer the threat against Britain from Hitler and the Germans, he wrote this in his diary:

"As I went to bed about 3 a.m., I was conscious of a profound sense of relief. At last I had the authority to give directions over the whole scene.

*I felt as I was walking with destiny, and that all my past life had been but a preparation for this hour and for this trial…*I thought I knew a good deal about it all, I was sure I should not fail." http://www.winstonchurchill.org

Did you catch that? ***Walking with destiny! All my past life had been but a preparation for this hour and for this trial!***

God has prepared assignments and has designed a work for you and I to accomplish. God has put destiny in your heart, which is His link to His eternal plan for us.

Destiny is defined as:

- Something that is to happen or has happened to a particular person or thing.
- The predetermined, usually inevitable or irresistible, course of events.
- The power or agency that determines the course of events. www.dictionary.com

In the book of Ephesians, the Apostle Paul says some key things that help us understand our journey and ultimately connect with our destiny.

"In Him also we have obtained an inheritance, being predestined according to the purpose of Him who works all things according to the counsel of His will, that we who first trusted in Christ should be to the praise of His glory" Ephesians 1:11-12, NKJV

"For we are His workmanship, created in Christ Jesus for good works, which God prepared beforehand that we should walk in them" Ephesians 2:10 NKJV

God has a predetermined course of events that He has designed for you and me.

When we came to Christ, God in His foreknowledge determined to set us up for success. We were to obtain an inheritance that provides all we need for the journey and that propels us to be the praise of His glory.

Unfortunately, many of us are like the brother in Luke 15 who was living in the Father's house, had access to all the Father's goods and relationship, and yet missed the Father's heart. We lack understanding of what is ours and develop an ungrateful spirit at the events that take place in our life.

God desires everyone to walk into their destiny and HE allows transitions to take place, to work into us the needed ingredients that will take us further than we could have gone before the transition.

Questions to Ponder

1. How have you felt God shaping your destiny?

2. Take time to think through your past experiences. Can you identify significant moments that you can see the hand of God in your journey?

LIFE'S TRANSITIONS

Recently, my sister's children have given her two little grandbaby boys and a little girl. It's such an exciting time in our family. For the first year, each month my nephew's wife posted a picture of Charlie next to the same pillow, it's amazing to see how much he has grown in just a short time.

Natural transitions occur every day! All around us we experience change and we don't even think about it; we just accept transitions as part of our lives. Here are a few that come to mind:

- A baby is born and moves through the stages of development.
- A young child grows to become a young man (1 Corinthians 13:11).

- A single person moves into dating and then marriage, where life's transitions then take on a whole new meaning.

- As married life takes hold, young couples want to move into parenthood.

- Eventually parenthood moves to the time of empty nesting and being grandparents.

- Retirement begins to loom and potential downsizing must be done for this time.

These are transitions that we've all come to expect as a normal part of life. Most people handle these changes easily with anticipation and joy.

What about other transitions that take place that are unexpected or unplanned?

Career changes – These could include job loss, lack of employment, being overlooked for promotion and being moved into an unexpected new role.

Life changes – Life changes may consist of an unexpected pregnancy, the death of a loved one, divorce and remarriage, financial and health issues.

Church changes – New leaders may take over from those who have served in the past. The church might implement a new vision and purpose. New people come into the church. Growing a church requires the ability to navigate through various transitions and changes.

God wants to expand our lives and calls us to greater stages of advancement. He wants to take each of us to another level!

God always has a purpose and call that He wants to position us for.

This positioning and development requires faith and trust in a Great God. *He wants to take us from glory to glory into the image of Christ 2 Corinthians 3:18. NKJV*

Each time a change or transition occurs there are many things that take place both internally and externally. Many of these changes are initiated beyond our control.

There are so many things happening behind the scenes that we are not aware of. God is orchestrating his plan for our lives and we need to be willing to TRUST HIM in this season. Accept that this is a season and it too will pass. God will move you forward as you embrace the place you find yourself in.

Questions to Ponder

Remember that transitions are designed to move us to a better place.

1. List the transitions you are going through right now.

2. What areas can you identify that you are currently growing in?

3. What areas can you identify that you need to grow in?

IT'S TIME TO CHANGE

Many times throughout my life I've been privileged to be in the presence of many great men and women of God who boldly declare the Word of God and speak what they hear HIM say. I have been moved to walk and wage warfare with the prophetic words that have come over my life, many times it was a witness & confirmation to what God was internally showing me, speaking to me in my devotions and highlighted by the conversations I was having. I have learned to trust HIS voice as I have walked through life.

Throughout the Bible, we see men and women of God having this type of relationship with the Lord hearing and obeying HIS voice, stepping out in faith not really knowing where they were going but obeying that still small voice.

In Genesis 12, we have such an encounter between God and Abraham.

Here the Lord clearly speaks to Abraham.

The Lord had said to Abram, "Leave your native country, your relatives, and your father's family, and go to the land that I will show you. I will make you into a great nation. I will bless you and make you famous, and you will be a blessing to others. I will bless those who bless you and curse those who treat you with contempt. All the families on earth will be blessed through you." So Abram departed as the Lord had instructed, and Lot went with him. Abram was seventy-five years old when he left Haran. Genesis 12:1-4 NKJV

In my experience there are at least 3 ways transitions are initiated in our lives: The voice of The Lord, dissatisfaction with your current situation and a God initiated interruption.

Each of these will be discussed in detail, however, before we look at them allow me to say: **The ultimate purpose in any type of transition is for God to move us to another place in our lives and to create a story of His redeeming power at work in our journey.**

His plan is to bring us to our destiny of being more like HIM and demonstrating this to all who would be watching our lives and to bring glory and honour to HIS great name!

- **The Voice of the Lord**

Sometimes the Lord will rock our world by speaking to our hearts and lives. This can be through a God thought, a specific scripture that jumps off the page, an inner awareness that the Holy Spirit is speaking, a prophetic word or a divine conversation that stirs your heart to explore new things.

The first time God spoke to Abraham He didn't tell him where to go, **He told Abraham where he couldn't stay**. God said, *"Leave your fathers house to a place I will show you."*

Like Abraham, sometimes we find ourselves in situations in which God refuses to tell us where to go but He only shares with us where we can't stay. These seasons reveal whether we will trust HIM as our guide more than we hunger to know our purpose.

Any time God speaks, we are required to listen and obey regardless of the personal risk or discomfort it may bring. Abraham listened and we are the benefactors today.

Whenever you decide to listen, obey and to make a change, the effects of that decision are generational in their impact. Your decisions will affect your sons, daughters and their children and their children's children.

Whenever God speaks, the key ingredient is **OBEDIENCE**. You may not have all the answers but God is looking to see if you will obey Him in Faith.

- **Dissatisfaction with Your Current Situation**

Our next character, Bartimaeus, did the same old thing everyday; he got up, had some breakfast, went to the same old place, sat out in the baking sun waiting for people to come, hoping they would be generous and make the day easier. That was the routine or life of Bartimaeus.

Mark 10:46-52 says,

Then they reached Jericho, and as Jesus and his disciples left town, a large crowd followed him. A blind beggar named Bartimaeus (son of Timaeus) was sitting beside the road. When Bartimaeus heard that Jesus of Nazareth was nearby, he began to shout, "Jesus, Son of David, have mercy on me!" "Be quiet!" many of the people yelled at him. But he only shouted louder, "Son of David, have mercy on me!" When Jesus heard him, he stopped and said, "Tell him to come here." So they called the blind man. "Cheer up," they said. "Come on, he's calling you!" Bartimaeus threw aside his coat, jumped up, and came to Jesus. "What do you want me to do for you?" Jesus asked. "My rabbi," the blind man said, "I want to see!" And Jesus said to him, "Go, for your faith has healed you." Instantly the man could see, and he followed Jesus down the road.

Bartimaeus was dissatisfied with his state of life. He had had enough. He wanted to see change!

Have you ever had one of those moments when you come to the realization that things are not going to change until you change or until you make a change?

To Bartimaeus this was just another day in which, due to the condition of his life, he was unable to see. His place of comfort was to beg. At this point, however, he was dissatisfied with this condition. He was hungry for a change!

Wherever you find yourself, good or bad, if you're open and hungry for change God can find you!

The walk of faith is one that is lived out in the ordinary activities of life but from a God perspective. God wants to invade the ordinary of your life so that you can encounter HIS extraordinary. God desires that you will always be ready to respond to Him.

Something was different in the noise of the crowd. Sometimes when one of your senses is hurting, your other ones compensate. Bartimaeus' ears were attentive and open. Bartimaeus heard a new sound. It was the One who could change His life walking among the crowd. His faith was stirred by the noise of the crowd.

Bartimaeus began to cry out! God plays no favorites. He looks for hungry and desperate people. **Earthly brokenness creates heavenly openness.** Times of transitions are always times when a greater cry for God is needed. You want Him to intervene and make things different.

The following verses emphasize God's response to our cry:

"The eyes of the LORD are on the righteous, and His ears are open to their cry" Psalm 34:15 NLT

"The righteous cry out, and the LORD hears, and delivers them out of all their troubles" Psalm 34:17 NLT

Desperation is often scorned and ridiculed by the masses. People will try to stop you from obtaining your encounter with God. You must be willing to press into the Kingdom to receive your encounter from God. Risk takers are not the norm and people will want to discourage you from your dreams and destiny. Real faith is always opposed to the play-it-safe mentality!

Bartimaeus cried out all the more! Increase your petition to God. Don't grow weary. Be determined! You will reap your reward.

"And let us not grow weary while doing good, for in due season we shall reap if we do not lose heart" Galatians 5:9 NLT

Throughout Scripture, we see men and women who, when they cried out to the Lord, He was always willing to respond to their cry.

At that moment of desperation Jesus stood still! What stops God in His tracks? Are you prepared to keep on asking, keep on seeking and keep on knocking until He takes notice?

"So I say to you, ask, and it will be given to you; seek, and you will find; knock, and it will be opened to you. For everyone who asks receives, and he who seeks finds, and to him who knocks it will be opened" Luke 11:9-10, NLT

There will come a moment in time when God will stop and take notice. It's not that He hasn't always noticed but HE is ready to act, the conditions are right, the heart is prepared for what He desires. Our role is to come to this place of desperation and willingly cry out to God.

There are a few things that the Lord required from Bartimaeus:

1. **Jesus commanded him to come** – God required a willingness to obey.

"By faith Abraham obeyed when he was called to go out to the place, which he would receive as an inheritance. And he went out, not knowing where he was going" Hebrews 11:10 NJKV

Obedience is the greatest quality that will bring you to your destiny.

When you set your heart to obey, you will experience a fresh touch to walk into your destiny.

2. **He threw off his cloak** – God required a willingness to leave the past behind.

Bartimaeus' cloak represented his lifestyle and behaviour—what he was known for before his encounter with Jesus and His mercy.

In times of transition, we need to be willing to walk from our past into our future. We need to be willing to let go of what we know and be willing to risk what we don't know. It is very easy for people and circumstances to continue to pull you back into your past; you must be willing to move forward regardless.

God desires us to leave everything to follow His destiny for our lives.

"It is very hard to fully step into your destiny while you are still holding onto your history. You must let go in order to lay a hold of..." Christine Caine

3. **Jesus tested his motives** — "What do you want Me to do for you?"

There seemed to be an obvious answer to this question, however, Jesus wanted to make sure Bartimaeus knew what he wanted. Jesus does the same with us in a time of transition. We need to know what we want Jesus to do for us.

Transition times are a time for us to refine our purpose and vision for our lives.

WHAT DO YOU WANT HIM TO DO FOR YOU?

At times, we must be willing to move beyond our comfort zones, cry out to God and get a fresh or new vision for our lives.

- **A God Initiated Interruption**

On Saturday August 10, 1985 I married the woman of my dreams. It was a wonderful hot summers day; we had a great honeymoon and arrived home ready to start our new life together. A few years later we decided to begin a family, 8 months went by and we were seeing no results. We decided to go to the doctor to see what was going on.

After a few tests, it was determined that I was born sterile. The report came back stating that we would need to find alternative ways to have a child and private adoption was suggested. I can tell you that this was a unique time in our brief life together, a transition was occurring.

We were faced with a number of questions: How was this going to define us? How would we respond to this? How would this affect our marriage and life together? How would this affect our faith in a great God?

Another Bible character named Moses was going about his day relegated to the backside of the desert due to a transition gone wrong. Off in the distance something caught his attention.

It's not everyday while in the backside of the desert do you see a burning bush; it was not normal.

Sometimes God will put before you something that is so amazing that you have to inquire further. It grips you and causes you to take action! God used this event to get his attention.

Moses was comfortable living his life in obscurity and failure. He was running from his destiny and purpose but that was all about to change.

Before you can enter into your destiny and purpose, many things in you heart will need to be addressed. Who are you? What will define you? Will life stay the same or will you be willing to move forward?

Exodus 3:10-14 says, "Come now, therefore, and I will send you to Pharaoh that you may bring My people, the children of Israel, out of Egypt." But Moses said to God, "Who am I that I should go to Pharaoh, and that I should bring the children of Israel out of Egypt?" So He said, "I will certainly be with you. And this shall be a sign to you that I have sent you: When you have brought the people out of Egypt, you shall serve God on this mountain."

Then Moses said to God, "Indeed, when I come to the children of Israel and say to them, 'The God of your fathers has sent me to you,' and they say to me, 'What is His name?' what shall I say to them?" And God said to Moses, "I AM WHO I AM." And He said, "Thus you shall say to the children of Israel, 'I AM has sent me to you.'" NKJV

God was calling Moses out of his lifestyle of wrong thinking and previous failure to another level.

He was calling him to kingship and authority done God's way. He was calling him to lead the nation of Israel into its destiny. All that Moses had gone through was for this time.

He would need to pull from all of his experiences, good and bad, for what was about to take place.

The transitions of faith always bring our identity into question. Who are we? Are we who man says we are? Are we what our circumstances say we are? Or are we who God says we are?

Moses questioned who he was. Moses was trained in the courts of Pharaoh as a king's son! This mindset got him to his current place of backside desert living. Earlier in his life, he had tried to make his destiny happen, unfortunately it was not God's time and it forced him to run in fear and failure. Fast forward 40 years later and now God was calling him into a life altering transition but this time he was unsure of what to do. His life circumstance had created a sense of insecurity for him, yet Moses was right where God needed him to be!

HE was RIGHT where GOD NEEDED him to be!

God had to remove the earthly kingdom mindset to replace it with HIS Kingdom mindset.

It's a mindset that depends and relies upon the character of GOD not on a self-motivated, proud and arrogant way of doing things but a God centered motivation.

Transitions will always help us to secure our proper identity in Christ. Most of us place our identity on what we do rather than on whose we are. God will use transitions as a time of stripping bare all that we have been defined by.

A time of transition is a crucial time in the life of a person or even the life of a church or an organization. This is when we are most vulnerable. We can be vulnerable to attack or drifting. Our identity and destiny are evaluated and possibly refined and refocused.

In a time of transition, crucial questions are asked: Who have I become? How did I get here? Is this who I really want to be? What will the next years of my life look like? Transitions require us to make key decisions that will determine what will play out in the next step of the journey.

Our identity must be firmly established in Christ and not in roles, function or position.

Transitions often create changes in those areas and if our identity is rooted in what we do or the position we hold, life can be very fragile. However, when rooted in Christ, a calm peace and assurance will cover our soul that God is in control and guiding us to something great.

The greatest compliment we can have is that God is with us and our identity is in HIM!

I'm happy to say that after 5 years of waiting for God to answer our cry, we became pregnant and 8 months later we had a precious little boy, Joshua Joel. On the day of his birth, as we stood in that hospital room crying and thanking God, our doctor just shook our hand and said, "this is a miracle, this is a miracle!"

That day as I stood holding my newborn son, I realized that God had done something amazing in our lives. He not only provided us with a precious gift, but He worked in us something deeper, richer and life changing. He brought us closer to Himself, helped us grow in our character and drew us closer to each other. Our faith, although tested, was established and strengthened. This test has defined us and made us better, not bitter.

Over the years we have been able to share our story and watch many lives touched, children birthed and people's faith increased to believe that God can take any season and work deeply, HIS plan and purpose. He is truly a faithful GOD!

Questions to Ponder

1. What initiated your point of transition?

2. How do you feel you are doing so far?

3. The next chapter we deal with the emotions involved in transition and change. List some of the emotions you have experienced so far. What are the most obvious? What are the ones that have taken you by surprise?

EMOTIONS, EMOTIONS, EMOTIONS

This past year some great friends decided to downsize and get ready for retirement in a few years. They purchased a new place and the renovations began, new paint, flooring and new updated furniture will make this place a great retirement home. As we talked through this transition, many emotions came to the surface. There was a lot of excitement for the future, planning the new colours and design, and the potential money they will save to do other things with their time in the future. Along with that was also, some apprehension as to whether this move will work after living in their family home for a very long time.

Whenever a transition occurs a wide assortment of emotions take place in our lives. We have to accept that our emotions are real and can't be denied. However, we can't stay living in those emotions. We need to move forward and continually keep a forward press in our lives. Philippians 3:20

In every transition, we will need to confront the element of **fear.** In a major transition in Joshua's life, his leader passed away and he was tasked to take the people into the Promise Land. God encouraged Joshua multiple times, *"Be strong and of good courage, do not be afraid or discouraged"* Joshua 1:6,7,9 NKJV. Fear can hold you back or can be confronted and propel you forward. Much can be said about the emotion of fear and it's ability to hinder and mock you in your destiny. Confront fear and a new boldness with come to your life. Allow fear to take hold and you will be limited and may miss Gods best for your next stage.

"At the threshold of every transition in our lives the devil sends a spirit of fear. Therefore be STRONG and VERY courageous!" Christine Caine

When in transition you can experience the emotion of **grief.**

Grief is defined as:

- Deep or intense sorrow or distress
- Something that causes keen distress or suffering
- Informal trouble or annoyance

A sense of loss at what you are leaving can be part of the season of transition. A willingness to work through this deep emotion will make the change easier and less stressful.

Grief should be dealt with as quickly as possible or you will be stuck in a holding pattern and miss the wonder of the moment.

This season can be a very vulnerable time in which the enemy can sow discouragement, disappointment and even despair in your soul. It is important to have a period of mourning and possibly a funeral. Letting go of the past will help you embrace the future!

For every new beginning there has to be an ending.

I would encourage you to seek out a trusted friend to share and unburden your heart. They can give you at the very least a listening ear, and probably will give you a fresh perspective.

"Your most valuable resource is your own heart. The greatest risk is becoming so tired, so discouraged, or so angry that your soul begins to shrivel." Sam Chand

Pain is inevitable when change is required. No one likes to change and particularly if it has been forced upon us. Pain can be a gift from God! It allows us to identify areas that need developing and require a touch from God. God is more concerned with our growth than our comfort! He wants to remove any debris in our hearts that will hinder us from moving forward into His purposes.

Change will require us to walk through a season of pain and discomfort but if we will embrace it God will polish us and make us like an arrow for His purposes.

Isaiah 49:2 states: "*In the shadow of His hand He has hidden Me,* ***and made Me a polished shaft****; In His quiver He has hidden Me.*" *NKJV*

Polish always carries with it the idea of purging or cleansing.

"Don't always try to get out of the situation until you get from the situation what God has hidden in it for you." Dale Bonner

Understand that, to go to the next level we have to allow change to take place; change will require saying no to certain things we have grown confortable with in our lives which are hindering us from moving forward.

When we say no to these things we are able to say YES to the important changes required to get us to our destiny. Pain will highlight what needs to go and what needs to change.

Perhaps the greatest negative emotion during transition will be **anger and bitterness.** These can be unexpected or may have been simmering for a long time but can have no place in your heart. Quickly snuff them out. When someone turns against you or you lose a loved one, it is easy to get angry or bitter. But Romans 8:28 states, "All things work together for good to those who love God and are called according to His purpose." (NKJV)

Determining to make daily decisions to forgive and keep clean records will go a long way to maintaining joy and excitement through the process of transition.

Joseph could have allowed anger and bitterness to take hold of his heart but he determined to stay pure and allow the hand of God to work in his life.

After many years of delay and hardship, he was promoted and met face to face with his brothers. He was able to share the following in Genesis 50:19-20: "*But Joseph said to them, "Do not fear, for am I in the place of God? As for you, you meant evil against me, but God meant it for good, to bring it about that many people should be kept alive, as they are today"* NKJV

Pain has a purpose! Allow God to work in you the necessary process in your time of transition and watch what He will do through you!

"When you're born you're like a key with no cuts in it. As you go through life, each wound, failure, hurt...cuts into that strip of metal. And one day there is a clear click- your pain has formed the key that slips into the lock & opens your future." T D Jakes – Devotional & Journal

The emotion of **failure** is an intense emotion that must be left at the foot of the cross. What could I have done better? If I had only done more! Why did we make that choice?

Your job loss, for example, may be devastating but God may be setting you up for future success.

A friend of mine lost a really good job; however, it actually turned out to be a blessing. He decided to keep a good attitude and not allow failure to take hold. He took a pay cut and went to a job that showed future benefits.

God was gracious and he is now fulfilling his destiny in a dream job and serving the Lord with the new skills he acquired. He would never have developed those skills without losing that initial job and keeping a right attitude through it all.

Disappointment with how life is turning out can drastically affect how we approach transition and change.

This can't be happening! This shouldn't be happening to me! Why me and not him? Unfortunately, life happens, changes and transitions come. The sooner we accept this, the more easily we can move toward what God has in store for us.

A friend said this to me one time: "Sometimes God has to harden the heart of Pharaoh to move a nation to their destiny."

It isn't always about you; it's about the purposes of God being unfolded that involve you and others. Everyone has an appointment with destiny; don't allow disappointment to sidetrack you and cause you to miss your appointment!

Misunderstanding is another emotion that can affect you while in transition, people can say or do hurtful things and this can be very disappointing. You can feel like you are being misunderstood and it's not fair or just. This is a time to trust in God! Each time misunderstanding takes place is an opportunity for God to shine and manifest His fruit in your actions and life. Take heart, Jesus was misunderstood and ridiculed.

Allow time to determine your position; keep moving toward your destiny laid out, and God will vindicate you.

Transitions are not always negative, **excitement and joy** will begin to develop in your heart as you embrace change. There will always be a certain level of excitement at new opportunities and new doors opening.

Transitions can be exciting times of our lives. They can breathe new hope, faith and love into relationships. They can produce new found joy in areas that may have grown stagnant. Faith begins to well up in your heart for new seasons of growth and increase. You will begin to find your purpose in a greater way and God begins to show up in profound ways.

There is ultimately the place in God called **Peace and Rest** Hebrews 4 says: *we need to be diligent or labour to enter rest*. Rest is a place where we place our trust in a great God.

We need to come to a place where we live from peace and rest in God.

He is willing to act on our behalf but we must be willing to be patient and restful.

EVERYONE NEEDS REST FOR THEIR SOUL - Our mind, will and emotions.

Mark 6:31 – *"And He said to them, "Come aside by yourselves to a deserted place and rest a while." NKJV*

Psalms 37:7 – *"Rest in the LORD, and wait patiently for Him…"NKJV*

Hebrews 4:8-11 – *"For if Joshua had given them rest, then He would not afterward have spoken of another day.* ***There remains therefore a rest for the people of God****. For he who has entered His rest has himself also ceased from his works as God did from His. Let us therefore be diligent to enter that rest, lest anyone fall according to the same example of disobedience." NKJV*

Rest is a promise from God given to every person of faith; it can be missed if we are not careful to live from faith. Rest always needs to be entered into as it doesn't always come natural to our lives; we need to make a conscious choice by faith to enter a state of rest. Rest can be hindered by disobedience and unbelief that resides in our hearts.

Having an ear to hear, eyes to see and a heart to understand is crucial to entering rest, it is a ceasing from works and a rejection of a performance mentality!

"REST is CRUCIAL to LONGEVITY"

When we spend time daily in God's presence, He breathes deeply into our souls and give us rest.

Exodus 33:14 - God's presence will go with us and give us rest.

Rest comes as we trust and depend upon the finished work of Christ.

All that HE accomplished is for my benefit and strength!

The book of Hebrews encourages us to be diligent to enter rest. Diligence means to use speed, to make every effort, to be prompt or earnest, give diligence to.

The Christian life is one of paradox; before we can advance we must learn to rest in Christ.

Our natural reason says - if we do not work or walk, how can we ever reach our goal? What can we attain without effort? How can we ever get anywhere if we do not move?

Christianity does not begin with the big "DO" but the big "DONE". All that we are ever going to do begins from and in Christ and what He has done.

A Heart at Rest!

- A heart at rest - is able to hear and receive key things that will shape who you are.
- A heart at rest – can discern clearly key moments in time that will set your course and destiny.
- A heart at rest - is able to hear the Holy Spirit's promptings to share or minister healing to someone, a neighbour and friend.

- A heart at rest is able to fight from a position of peace rather than strife and conflict.
- A heart at rest – is empowered and dependent on the Holy Spirit's work in your life.
- A heart at rest moves in the rhythms of Grace.

"The ability to calm your soul and wait before God is one of the most difficult things in the Christian life. Our old nature is restless…the world around us is frantically in a hurry. But a restless heart usually leads to a reckless life." Warren Wiersbe

"Return to you rest O my soul, For the Lord has dealt bountifully with you." Psalm 116:7 NKJV

JESUS wants you to encounter HIM and ENTER HIS REST!

Questions to Ponder

1. What emotion(s) has been the most intense in this time?

2. What steps have you taken to work through this stage?

3. Find a trusted friend to share your emotions with and make sure that these are not holding you back.

DECISIONS, DECISIONS, DECISIONS

A number of years ago, I took a group of high school students white-water rafting on the Ottawa Valley River. It was an amazing time connecting with these great kids and enjoying the rapids.

On our first day, we had to sign a waiver that totally made us aware "we weren't in Kansas anymore." This was serious! Our lives could be at stake!

We then went through a series of training exercises and instruction time. Our guide was excellent and we felt somewhat safe. As we got onto the water, we began getting use to the raft and learning how to work together as a team. Then came the first rapid. It was a small rapid and we seemed to move through it effortlessly. "Let's keep going" was the cry! Now, these guys are smart. They take you through a bunch of small rapids before they launch you into the biggest rapids you have ever seen. They do this to build up your confidence, stamina and team building skills.

Along the way, we stopped for some swimming and horsing around. Prior to the last major rapid, they stopped upstream and walked us to a lookout point so we could see other groups go down. This is not for the fainthearted. This is also the time when you can opt out of going down this particular rapid, some decided they didn't want to go further. You could see the other rafts go down through the rapids, occasionally turn over, and send people flying. This is where all the training and preparation comes in handy. You're still scared out of your mind, but you tell yourself you're ready.

We got back in the raft, and the guide proceeded to walk us through how to approach this mighty behemoth of a rapid. Then off we went. I'm happy to say no one was lost and we did not capsize.

A great time was had by all and many great memories were made.

The journey is like that. We prepare and train when we have small rapids to face. Each one of them builds our confidence and skill. Then we face the BIG one. What we have now learned through experience and trusting the people with us will determine how we handle major transitions in our lives. Will we get through them or will we capsize? Will we decide to opt out or will we have courage to move forward?

With every transition there are a number of decisions that need to be made if we are going to navigate through this time.

1. **Choose to respond.** AM I WILLING?

Abram departed; Bartimaeus began to shout; Moses trusted God and Joshua took courage.

Every transition requires a willingness to respond. Our task is to be willing to go, stay, trust God or resolve to be courageous. Every step of faith requires a decision to respond. When you are faced with change, be bold, look it in the face and say I'm ready! I'm willing!

This one decision will take you further than you can imagine.

2. **Choose to leave the past behind.** WHAT AM I WILLING TO LEAVE BEHIND?

Abram left his family and country; Bartimaeus left his coat; and Moses left his insecurity, wrong thinking and failure.

Faith will always challenge us to move beyond our comfort zones.

Philippians 3:7 "But what things were gain to me, these I have counted loss for Christ. Yet indeed I also count all things loss for the excellence of the knowledge of Christ Jesus my Lord, for whom I have suffered the loss of all things, and count them as rubbish, that I may gain Christ" NKJV

Each day I am reminded of the need to walk away from the past.

Your past should not define you but it should shape you into being a person who is determined to succeed by holding the hand of God as you walk out your journey.

You will need to keep a short record and allow a forgiving spirit to be in your heart.

3. **Choose to trust in a good and faithful God.** AM I ABLE?

Psalm 37:5-7a "Commit your way to the Lord, Trust also *in Him, And He shall bring it to pass. He shall bring forth your righteousness as the light, and your justice as the noonday. Rest in the Lord, and wait patiently for Him to act" NKJV*

It is God's business to fulfill our faith. It is His timing that matters. Our plans and schemes mean nothing before a mighty God. He is the author and finisher of our faith. We must be willing to wait for Him to act.

4. **Choose to sanctify yourself.**

Joshua 3:5 "And Joshua said to the people, 'Sanctify yourselves, for tomorrow the Lord will do wonders among you'" NKJV

"Sanctify" doesn't have to be a difficult word to understand. It basically means to be clean. Now I'm not saying you need to take a bath, but you do need to take time to allow the Holy Spirit to examine your heart.

Psalm 139:23-24 "Search me, O God, and know my heart; Try me, and know my anxieties; and see if there is any wicked way in me, and lead me in the way everlasting" NKJV

Whenever a time of transition or change is upon your life, it is always refreshing to allow the Holy Spirit to touch your heart and speak.

You want to make sure that, as you are moving toward your destiny, you clear the way and allow nothing to stop what God wants to do.

As I began my most recent transition, I spent a few days waiting on the Lord asking Him to make sure that there was no residue in my life. The Lord was gracious to me and showed me that I had allowed certain mindsets into my life and lies about who He was. The biggest lie was that I didn't believe He was in control. Once I surrendered that lie and declared HIS lordship, a great peace and joy flooded my soul. I was filled with the sense that God was deeply in control of everything.

5. Choose to keep a spirit of gratitude in your heart.

Philippians 4:6 states, "Rejoice in the Lord always and again I say rejoice. Be anxious for nothing!" (NKJV)

Attitude is everything in the midst of change and transition. A spirit of gratitude is vital to any season of transition, keeping a positive grateful heart will help when difficult times come.

6. Choose to celebrate the journey.

Life's not that hard! The Christian life is all about the journey. Allow God to continue to refine and define your character, attitude and motives in the midst of transition. God is always more interested in developing and making you into the person HE wants you to be, a person who can handle the next part of the amazing journey God has planned.

Proverbs 4:23 states: "Always keep your heart right at all times" NLT

This is a powerful thought as your heart will be tested in this season and must be guarded at all times.

The enemy wants to sow seeds of unbelief, disappointment and potentially bitterness into your life. Guard your Heart.

Never allow the fear of man or the approval of man to guide you or influence you.

Remember, it's your journey and you're the only one who can determine the steps you will take.

The journey will always require faith, perseverance, honesty, flexibility and openness to what God would do. There is no other way to live life. Many people get tied up in the "what ifs". What if this happens? What if I can't? What if something goes wrong?

The journey requires a willingness to be led by the Holy Spirit each day.

All transitions will have trials, testing, disappointments and setbacks. Keep Going!

Stay connected to the Lord, other people and the local church. One of the greatest principles I have learned is the safety of friends and being planted in a local church.

I believe this has helped me weather some difficult storms knowing people are there to support, pray and rejoice with us on the journey.

Always take a few people with you on the journey – don't go it alone! I have many friends that I have known for 30, 25, 20 and 15 years that I get to do life with. It is a great joy to continually see our progress over the years.

Transitions require you to speak faith and hope into other people's journey, and to demonstrate love. I believe the greatest quality you can possess is to be an encourager. I want to encourage you to be someone who deposits encouragement in the hearts of people around you and urge them on to continue the race Jesus started them on. You will never be disappointed that you had a hand in helping someone get to their destiny and purpose.

7. Choose to honour those who have helped you so far.

Every person needs people who will champion him or her when they are in this season. We all need special friends who encourage and believe in God's dreams for us.

We also need to honour the investment of those who have impacted our lives. God will honour you as you honour and speak well about the people who invested in your life both negatively or positively.

8. Choose to open your heart to new opportunities, new doors and new connections.

God desires that you be willing to expand your heart to receive what He would want to bring to you. In my own time of transition, I have met some tremendous people of faith and success.

I have been able to travel to places I would have never thought possible prior to making the decision to obey the Lord.

9. Choose to allow the fruit of the Holy Spirit to flourish in your life.

Galatians 5:22: "The fruit of the Spirit is love, joy, peace, patience, kindness, goodness, faithfulness, gentleness and self-control." NLT

During times of transition, the Lord wants to go deeper in your life. He wants to develop more of Himself in your heart and mind.

10. Choose to Dream

During this season, take time to allow God to birth new dreams or refine old ones as you move into the future. Dreams are the language of the Holy Spirit, allow Him to renew the dreams of your youth!

11. Choose to Stay the Course

"Don't doubt in darkness what God has spoken in light." When you are frustrated with times of inactivity and waiting, keep the faith (Philippians 1:6). God is in the darkness, He is working out His will for your life, we need to stay the course and trust the process.

Trust God's timing. In every transition, timing is a huge issue. God's timing is always perfect. There is a set time for the manifestation of your life, even creation eagerly groans with anticipation of the manifestation of the sons of God. Focus on doing what you know is right to do and trust Him to be faithful to complete what He started.

12. Choose to be Watchful

Watch for weariness. It can be easy to become weary in the midst of transition. However, it's in these moments you can open your mind up to satanic attack and get off course. Guard your heart.

Don't allow perceived injustices and mistreatment to cause bitterness in your heart. God is in control. Watch for little foxes. Little things, if not checked, can lead to bigger issues. Make sure they are dealt with in a timely manner.

13. Choose Christ Daily

Renew your mind and heart each day with God's Word and Spirit. Your daily time with God is important in the midst of transitions, particularly tough ones. By setting your face to seek Him each day you are letting God know that He is most important in your life and day.

14. Patience, patience, patience!

Allow patience to develop. Patience is the ability to stand under the pressure of the moment. Patience and endurance help long distance runners accomplish what, to many, seem impossible. they have learned to press through and stay patient. They have allowed courage & patience to dispel discouragement and fatigue.

Isaiah 40:31 states: But those who wait on the LORD Shall renew [their] strength; They shall mount up with wings like eagles, They shall run and not be weary, They shall walk and not faint. NKJV

Questions to Ponder

1. What decisions have you been postponing that you need to make today?

2. What are you dreaming about that you need to set you heart toward?

3. Are there any areas you need to be watchful in right now?

ENJOY THE JOURNEY

I hope these thoughts have brought some clarity to your journey and allowed you to gauge how you are doing in the midst of your transition, whether great or small. God desires to take you to your destiny and part of that is navigating the transitions that come in life.

I recently was asked to write a short version of my time of transition and any experiences that took place. I have included this here to recap what the Lord has done and continues to do.

"Three years ago I was in the midst of the biggest change of my life, I was leaving a job of 16 years that I loved and about to embark on a new adventure with no certainty or security. Security had not been an issue in my life, I've always had work and been able to provide for my family.

However, leaving a job to go to follow a dream was not a normal occurrence in my life and would require a new set of parameters of thinking and living.

Over the years life had gotten busy with many areas of responsibility crowding in, each area taking time and precious internal resources along the way. I can't say I was empty but I certainly was feeling drained, a little fearful and in need of an encounter with Jesus for this next stage of the journey.

I scheduled some time away out west and began to seek HIM. Most of the week was a rush of activity, however, each day HE began to speak to me, encouraging my heart the direction I was on was the right direction, to stay with it and to TRUST HIM!

One morning I was having my devotions in a prayer chapel when I noticed a guy taking communion. I thought I haven't had communion in a while "why not?" As I took the cup and wafer I proceeded to rehearse in my mind Jesus' words. "As often as you drink this cup and eat this bread you remember me." I stopped and said out loud – Jesus, I remember you!

At that moment HIS PRESENCE invaded the place I stood, my heart & body began to feel HIS embrace! It felt like we were standing face to face with each other. I began to experience HIS deep LOVE pour into me like warm oil. Tears began to flow and I heard HIS promptings.

I LOVE YOU! Everything will be fine! I'm with YOU! TRUST ME! You're a person of VALUE! YOU are LOVED!

In the next 15 or 20 minutes all of life seemed to stop and my encounter with JESUS' LOVE began to change me internally. A deeper sense of security and peace flooded my mind and heart. HE was in CONTROL of my life. The busyness of the years began to fade away and a new rhythm of HIS GRACE started to take place in my heart. Fear of the future disappeared and FAITH, HOPE & LOVE began to take place deep in my core. I was changed! HIS LOVE had captured my heart again!

It's been 3 years since that moment and it's as real today as it was then. HE LOVES me! Everything is Fine! HE is with me! I TRUST HIM! I am a Person of VALUE! I am LOVED!

I believe that everyone reading this book can experience the Peace, Faith, Hope and Love that I felt that day, remember, God is for you! He's on your side! He is in control of the outcomes of our lives.

Allow me to finish by quoting a story from Patrick Morley's book, *The Second Half for the Man in the Mirror*. I would like to use this in relation to transition.

> "The beautiful mysterious St. John's River meanders through Central Florida not far from where we live. Near the headwaters the river runs swift, but the waters slow as the river deepens as the journey lengthens. Halfway to its final destination, the river opens into a huge lake. Without its two banks, the river has no direction. The waters spread out and barely moves. Each droplet of water entering the mouth of this lake travels a different course.

> But this is not the Dead Sea, so eventually two riverbanks gather the waters, and the river once again runs steady." (The Second Half of the Man in the Mirror)

Transition is like coming into that lake. You can seem to lose speed and direction. Life can suddenly take on a whole other meaning and you may feel like you're drifting, drowning or left to fend for yourself.

A transition can also be a time of tranquility and peace—a time to find yourself and recalibrate your life, a time to slow down and take stock of where you have been, where you are and where you need to go.

I would encourage you not to rush this time; you will eventually get back out into the river and move steadily along.

Transition can be a time of rest, reflection and determining your next steps.

It is a time to set the course for your destiny.

"Remember: Because God is good, your life will not turn out like you planned—it will turn out even better"

(Pat Morley, *Second Half for the Man in the Mirror*).

BIBLIOGRAPHY

TRUST THE GPS
Page 2 - www.dictionary.com

HOLY SPIRIT INTENTIONS
Page 6 - Joey Bonifacio – The Promise No One Wants.

WALKING WITH DESTINY
Page 10-11 - www.winston-churchill-leadership.com
Page 11 www.dictionary.com

IT'S TIME TO CHANGE
Page 23 - Christine Caine Quote
Chapter 6
Page 30 - Christine Caine Quote
Page 30 www.dictionary.com
Page31 - Sam Chand – Leadership Pain Quote
Page32 - Dale Bonner – Leadership Pain Quote
Page 33 - T D Jakes – Devotional & Journal Quote
Page 38 - Warren Wiersbe Quote

DECISIONS, DECISION, DESIONS
Page 49-50 – Patrick Morely – The Second Half of the man in the Mirror
Page 50 - Patrick Morely – The Second Half of the man in the Mirror

ABOUT THE AUTHOR

Gary has been involved in ministry for over 30 years, most recently serving on staff at Living Hope Christian Assembly in Hamilton, Ontario for 16 years. Gary has a genuine love for people of all ages, preaches with humor, inspiration and a prophetic touch. His desire is to see people come to Christ, encourage leaders and strengthen churches. Gary has been married to Sheila since 1985 and has one son, Joshua and a new daughter-in-law, Melissa.

Made in the USA
Middletown, DE
09 April 2016